How Do Penguins Survive the Cold?

Mary Ann Hoffman

New York

Published in 2009 by The Rosen Publishing Group, Inc.
29 East 21st Street, New York, NY 10010

Copyright © 2009 by The Rosen Publishing Group, Inc.

All rights reserved. No part of this book may be reproduced in any form without permission in writing from the publisher, except by a reviewer.

Book Design: Michael J. Flynn

Photo Credits: Cover © Francois Etienne du Plessis/Shutterstock; pp. 3, 4, 6, 7 (background), 8, 9 (background), 11, 12, 14 (background), 15, 16, 17 (background), 19, 20, 22 (background), 23, 24 © Peter Wey/Shutterstock; pp. 5, 9 (top right) © Jeff Goldman/Shutterstock; p. 7 © Fred Kamphues/Shutterstock; pp. 9 (left and bottom right), 10 © Nik Niklz/Shutterstock; p. 9 (middle right) © Nicolaas/Shutterstock; p. 13 © (penguin) © Christian Musat/Shutterstock; p. 13 (killer whale) © Khoo Si Lin/Shutterstock; p. 13 (leopard seal) © Jan Martin Will/Shutterstock; p. 14 © Raldi Somers/Shutterstock; p. 17 © Doug Allan/The Image Bank/Getty Images; p. 18 © Susan Flashman/Shutterstock; p. 21 (penguin hopping) © Joe McDonald/Visuals Unlimited/Getty Images; p. 21 (inset) © Brian L. Lambert/Shutterstock; p. 22 © Gerald Kooyman/Corbis.

Library of Congress Cataloging-in-Publication Data

Hoffman, Mary Ann, 1947-
　How do penguins survive the cold? / Mary Ann Hoffman.
　　　p. cm. -- (Real life readers)
　Includes index.
　ISBN: 978-1-4042-8007-6
　6-pack ISBN: 978-1-4042-8009-0
　ISBN 978-1-4358-2969-5 (library binding)
　1. Penguins--Juvenile literature. 2. Penguins--Adaptations--Juvenile literature. I. Title.
　QL696.S473H626 2009
　598.47--dc22
                                        2008036907

Manufactured in the United States of America

Contents

What Is a Penguin?	4
Cold Water	6
Kinds of Penguins	8
Where Do Penguins Live?	11
What Do Penguins Eat?	12
Do Penguins Communicate?	15
Emperor Penguins	16
Fairy Penguins	19
Rockhopper Penguins	20
Special Birds	22
Glossary	23
Index	24

What Is a Penguin?

A penguin is a bird. Like all birds, it has wings, feathers, two legs, and a bill. It lays eggs. However, although penguins have wings, they don't fly. They use their wings for swimming! Many penguins spend over half their lives swimming and hunting in very cold water. They **waddle** when they walk, and they need to hop to get over large rocks. Penguins also like to slide down icy hills on their stomachs.

Penguins have short legs, and they stand very straight.

Cold Water

Penguins are built for swimming. They have heavy bones that help them stay underwater. Their wings are short and stiff, and they use them like paddles to swim quickly. They use their webbed feet to push themselves through the water. Their long tails guide their direction.

Penguins swim in water that is usually very cold. Penguins have two **adaptations** that help keep them warm. They have a thick **layer** of fat called blubber under their skin. They also have special feathers that keep the cold water away from their skin.

This penguin has its wings spread wide as it swims through the water.

PENGUINS

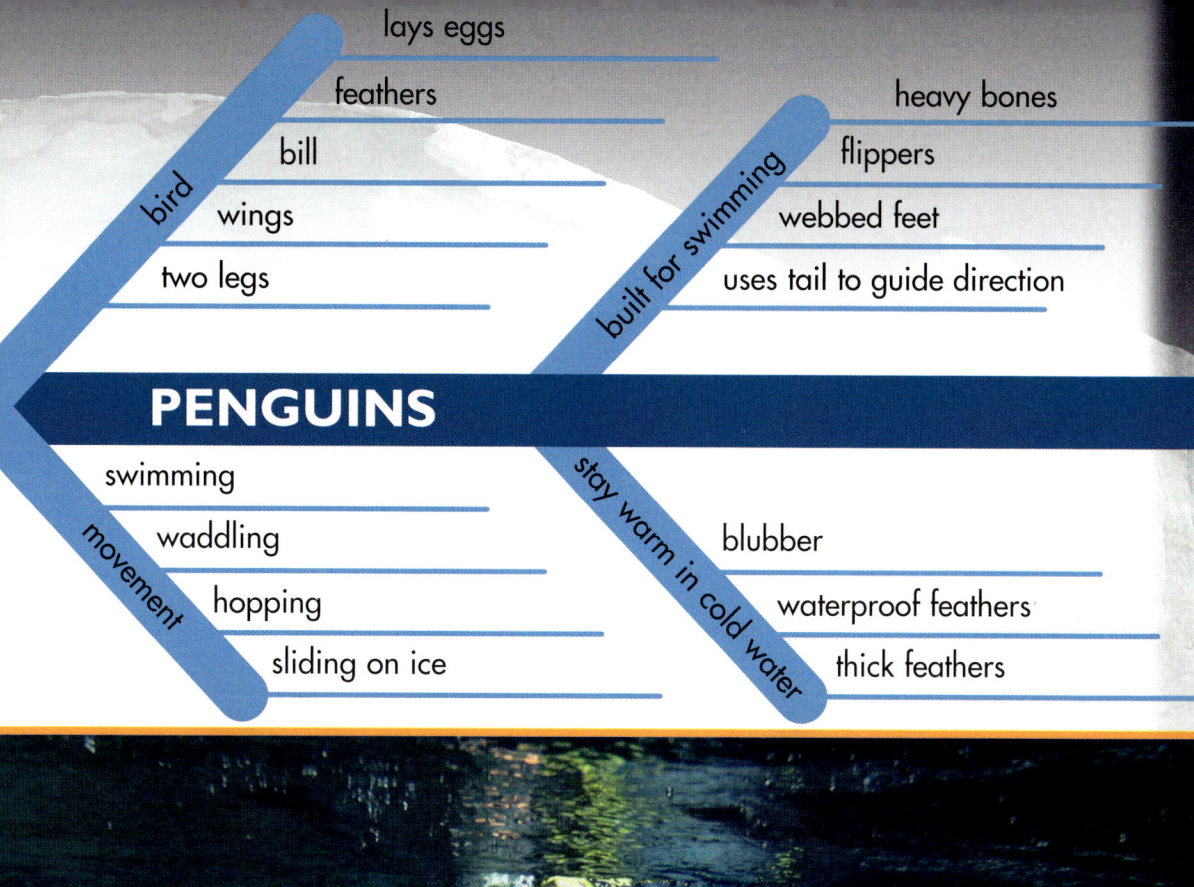

bird
- lays eggs
- feathers
- bill
- wings
- two legs

built for swimming
- heavy bones
- flippers
- webbed feet
- uses tail to guide direction

movement
- swimming
- waddling
- hopping
- sliding on ice

stay warm in cold water
- blubber
- waterproof feathers
- thick feathers

7

Kinds of Penguins

There are seventeen kinds of penguins. They come in many different sizes. All penguins have black or darkly colored backs and white fronts. Some have colored feathers on their chest and head. They can also have colored bills, feet, and eyes.

Some penguins have long, sharp bills. They eat fish. Other penguins have thick bills that they use to catch **krill**. All penguins have strong, webbed feet with claws.

> Look at the three penguins on the right. How are they the same? How are they different?

Where Do Penguins Live?

Wild penguins live south of the **equator**. Many live around **Antarctica**, where it's very cold most of the year. Galápagos (guh-LAH-puh-guhs) penguins live near the equator where it's usually warm. However, the water around the Galápagos Islands is cold.

Penguins spend most of their lives at sea. They nest on islands and **ice floes**, and along coasts, far away from animals that might harm their eggs and young.

> Penguins live in large groups called colonies. Some colonies have millions of penguins!

What Do Penguins Eat?

Penguins eat **shrimp**, crabs, squid, fish, and krill. Some penguins catch and eat food near the water's surface. Others dive deep into the ocean for food. Penguins catch their food with their bills. Penguins don't have teeth. They swallow their food whole as they swim.

While searching for food, penguins keep watch for enemies such as killer whales. Some animals attack unguarded penguin eggs.

Leopard seals hide under ice floes and wait for penguins to dive into the water. Then they attack.

killer whale

leopard seal

13

Do Penguins Communicate?

Can you think of ways that you **communicate** with others? Maybe you talk to your friend, or smile when you hear a joke. How do you think penguins communicate?

Penguins communicate with sounds and motions. They tell each other where they are and warn of danger. Penguins use their voices to make sounds. They bob their heads and wave their wings. They clean and smooth their feathers. These are all ways of talking.

> Here are three penguins that look as if they are out for a walk. What do you think they might be communicating to each other?

Emperor Penguins

Emperor penguins, the largest penguins, live on the coast of Antarctica. They can grow to 4 feet (122 cm) tall and weigh up to 100 pounds (45 kg). They can dive more than 1,000 feet (305 m) into the ocean.

In the winter, the mother emperor penguin lays one egg. She gives it to the father and goes into the ocean to feed. The father holds the egg on top of his feet and tucks it into a special pouch. After about 2 months, a chick **hatches**. The father doesn't eat during this time. He's too busy keeping the chick safe.

> **Emperor penguins can live about 20 years, which is the longest of all penguins.**

Fairy Penguins

Fairy penguins are the smallest penguins. They live in warmer water near Australia and New Zealand. Most are about 16 inches (41 cm) tall and weigh about 2.2 pounds (1 kg).

Fairy penguins build nests in the ground under rocks. The mother penguin lays two eggs. Both parents take turns keeping the eggs warm. During the daytime, they take turns swimming into the ocean to feed. At night, they both return to the nest. When the chicks hatch, the parents bring food to them.

> Fairy penguins are gray-blue and have white stomachs. They are sometimes called blue penguins.

Rockhopper Penguins

Rockhopper penguins live on islands around Antarctica. They are **crested** penguins, which means they have brightly colored feathers on their heads. Rockhoppers got their name because they hop over the rocks that make up the islands where they live.

Rockhoppers make their nests in rocky places. The mother lays two eggs. The father sits on the eggs to keep them warm while the mother finds food. When rockhopper chicks are about 4 weeks old, groups of them gather together for warmth while their parents hunt for food.

> **Rockhoppers have long yellow feathers that look like eyebrows!**

	emperor penguin	fairy penguin	rockhopper penguin
how it looks	largest penguin	smallest penguin	brightly colored feathers on head
where it lives	Antarctica	Australia, New Zealand	islands around Antarctica
how many eggs it lays	one	two	two
which parent tends the eggs	father	both	father

Special Birds

Penguins can't fly, but they're great swimmers. The unusual shape of their bodies helps them swim. Their feathers make them look like they're wearing a dark suit and white shirt. They walk with a waddle and group together for work and play.

Penguins are special birds!

Glossary

adaptation (aa-dap-TAY-shun) A part or action of a type of animal that helps them stay alive.

Antarctica (ant-AHRK-tih-kuh) The large land mass around the South Pole of Earth.

communicate (kuh-MYOO-nuh-kayt) To share knowledge or feelings.

crested (KREHS-tuhd) Having a tall growth of hair or feathers on the head.

equator (ih-KWAY-tuhr) An imaginary line around the middle of Earth that separates it into two parts, northern and southern.

hatch (HACH) For a baby animal to break out of an egg.

ice floe (EYS FLOH) A large sheet of floating ice.

krill (KRIHL) Tiny ocean animals that penguins and other ocean animals eat.

layer (LAY-uhr) One thickness of something laying over or under another.

shrimp (SHRIMP) A small animal with ten legs that lives in water.

waddle (WAH-duhl) To walk with short, swaying steps.

23

Index

A
adaptations, 6
Antarctica, 11, 16, 20, 21
Australia, 19, 21

B
bill(s), 4, 7, 8, 12
blubber, 6, 7

C
chick(s), 16, 19, 20
cold water, 4, 6, 7
communicate, 15

E
eat, 8, 12, 16
egg(s), 4, 7, 11, 12, 16, 19, 20, 21
emperor penguin(s), 16, 21
enemies, 12

F
fairy penguin(s), 19, 21
feathers, 4, 6, 7, 8, 15, 20, 21, 22
feed, 16, 19
flippers, 7
food, 12, 19, 20

G
Galápagos penguins, 11

H
heavy bones, 6, 7

I
ice floes, 11

N
New Zealand, 19, 21

P
paddles, 6

R
rockhopper penguin(s), 20, 21

S
swim(ming), 4, 6, 7, 12, 19, 22

W
webbed feet, 6, 7, 8
wings, 4, 6, 7, 15

Due to the changing nature of Internet links, The Rosen Publishing Group, Inc., has developed an online list of Web sites related to the subject of this book. This site is updated regularly. Please use this link to access the list: http://www.rcbmlinks.com/rlr/pengu

FEAST FOR 10

CATHRYN FALWELL

Macmillan
McGraw-Hill

 **Macmillan
McGraw-Hill**

Macmillan/McGraw-Hill
A Division of The McGraw-Hill Companies
Two Penn Plaza, New York, NY 10121

This edition is printed in arrangement with Clarion Books, an imprint of Houghton Mifflin Company.

Copyright © 1993 by Cathryn Falwell.
All rights reserved.

No part of this publication may be reproduced or distributed in any form or by any means, or stored in a database or retrieval system, without the prior written consent of the publisher, including, but not limited to, network storage or transmission, or broadcast for distance learning.

Printed in the United States of America

ISBN 0-02-197821-2/Pre-K

2 3 4 5 6 7 8 9 (109) 10 09 08 07

For
my family

in
loving memory
of
my grandmothers

Willie Mae McMullen Chauvin
and
Evelyn Haning Falwell

who often made
feasts for plenty

1 one cart into the grocery store

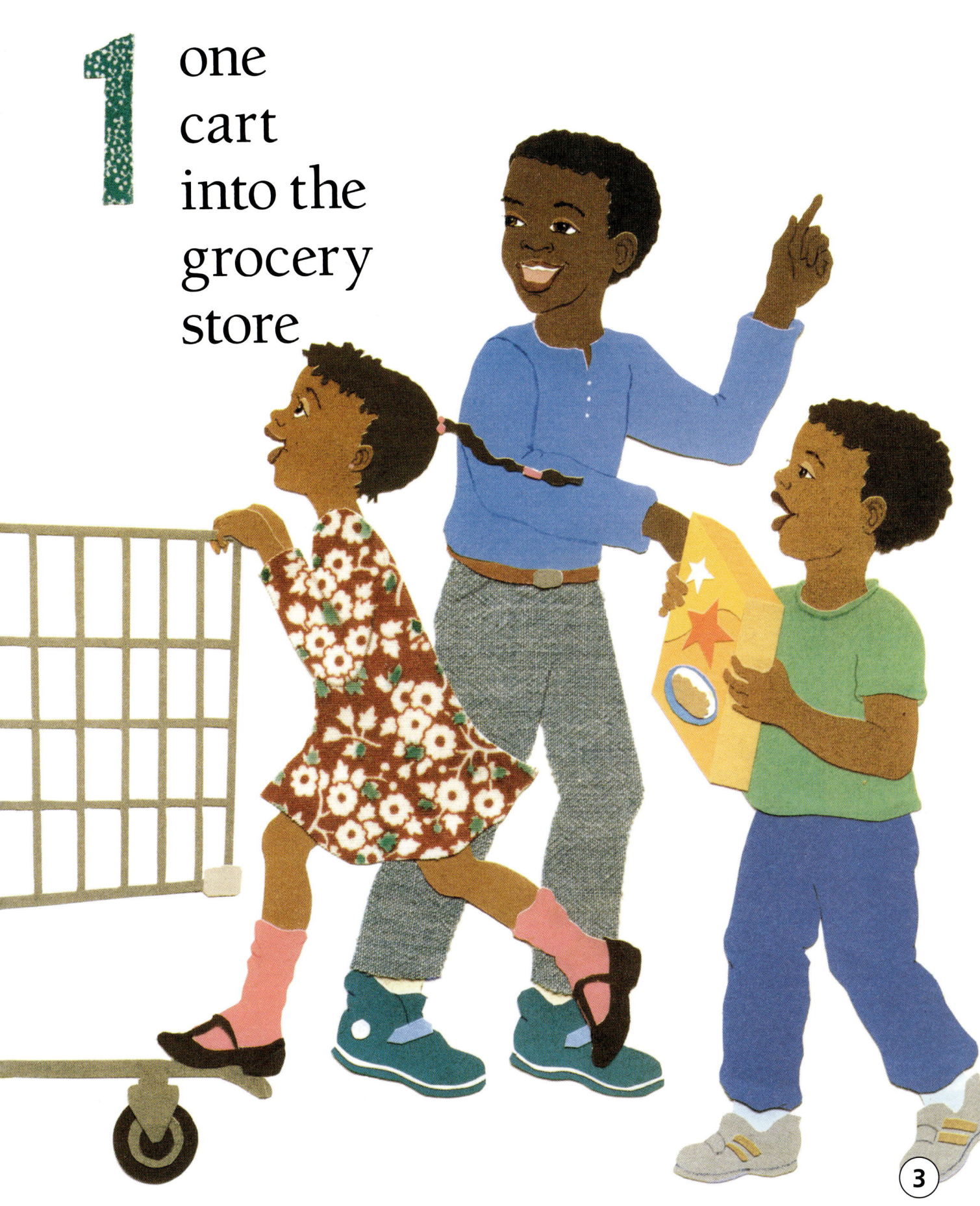

2 two pumpkins for pie

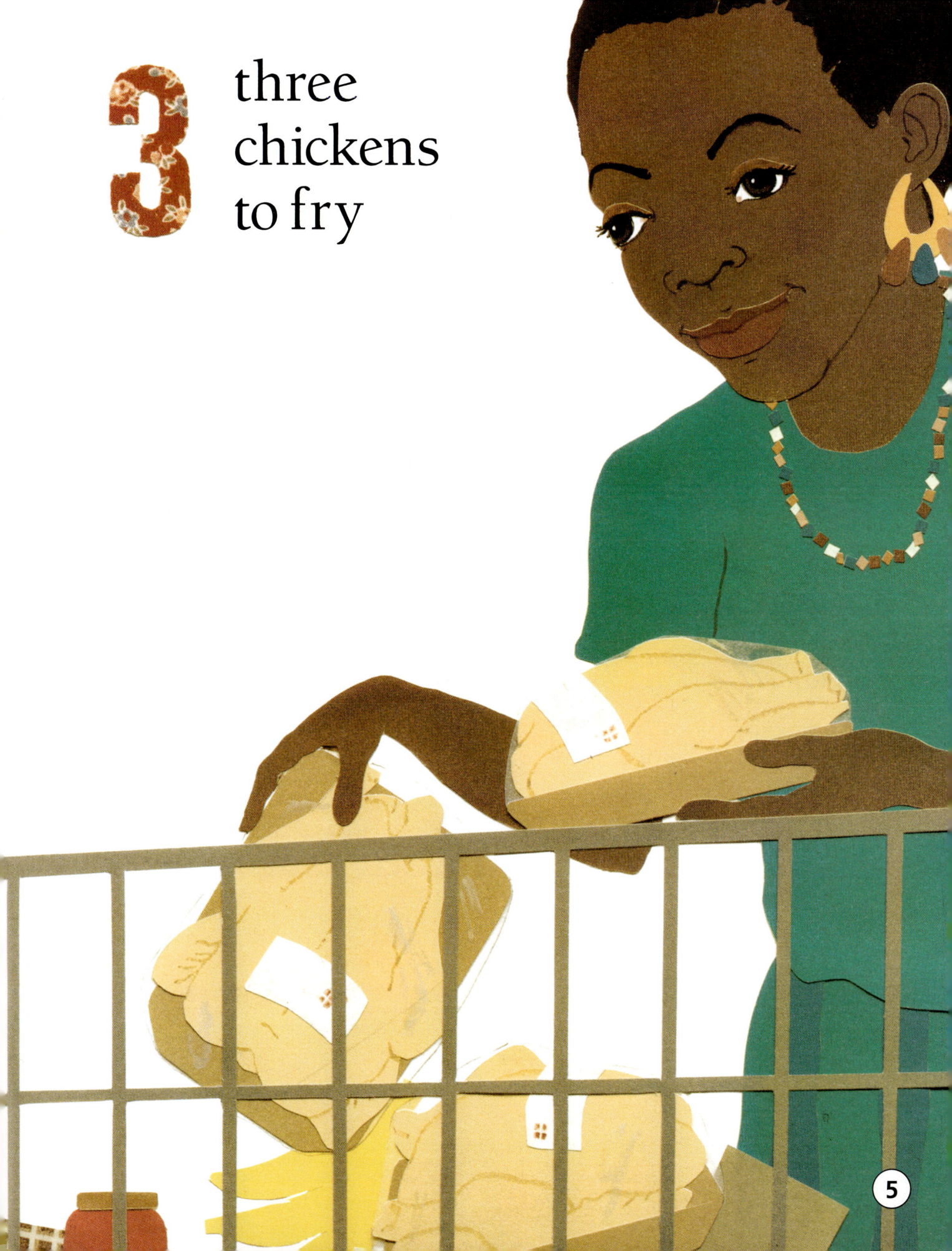

3 three chickens to fry

4

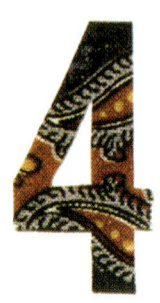

four
children
off to
look for
more

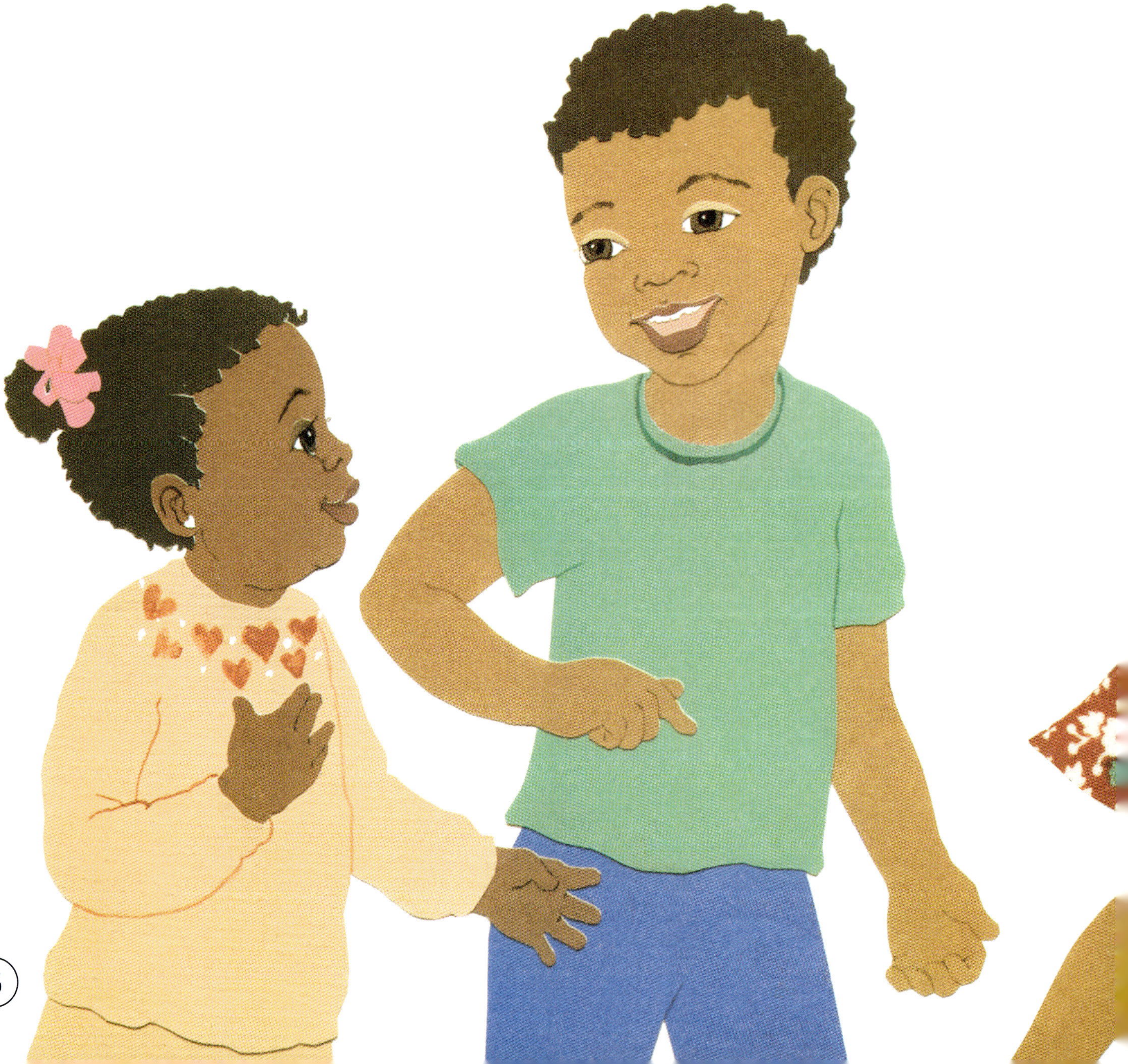

5 five kinds of beans

6 six bunches of greens

7 seven
dill pickles
stuffed in
a jar

8 eight
ripe
tomatoes

9 nine plump potatoes

10 ten hands help to load the car

15

Then . . .

1 one car home from the grocery store

17

2 two will look

3 three will cook

20

4 four
will
taste
and ask
for
more

5 five empty cans

6 six pots and pans

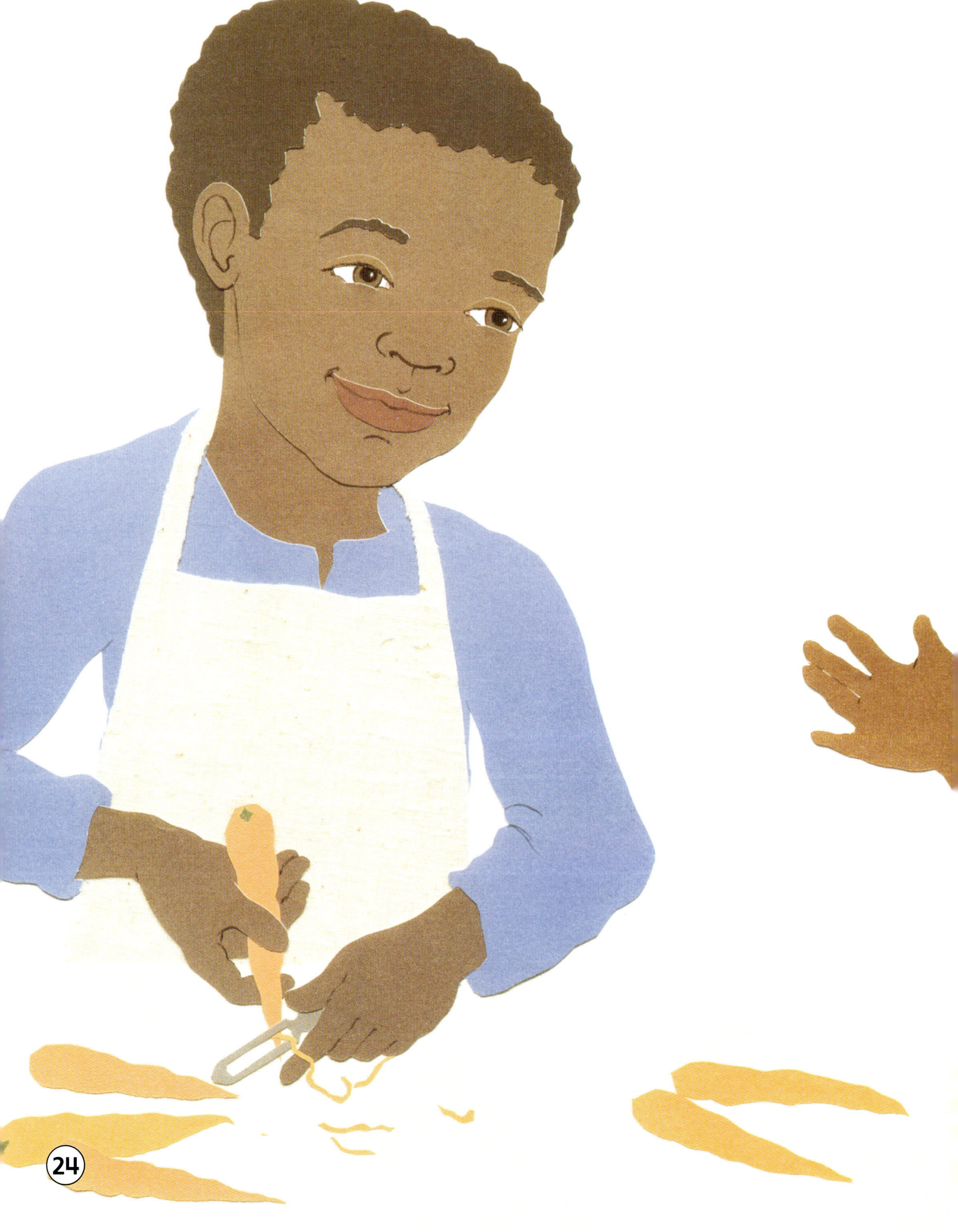

7 seven more carrots to wash and peel

8 eight platters down

9 nine chairs around

28

10 ten hungry folks to share the meal!

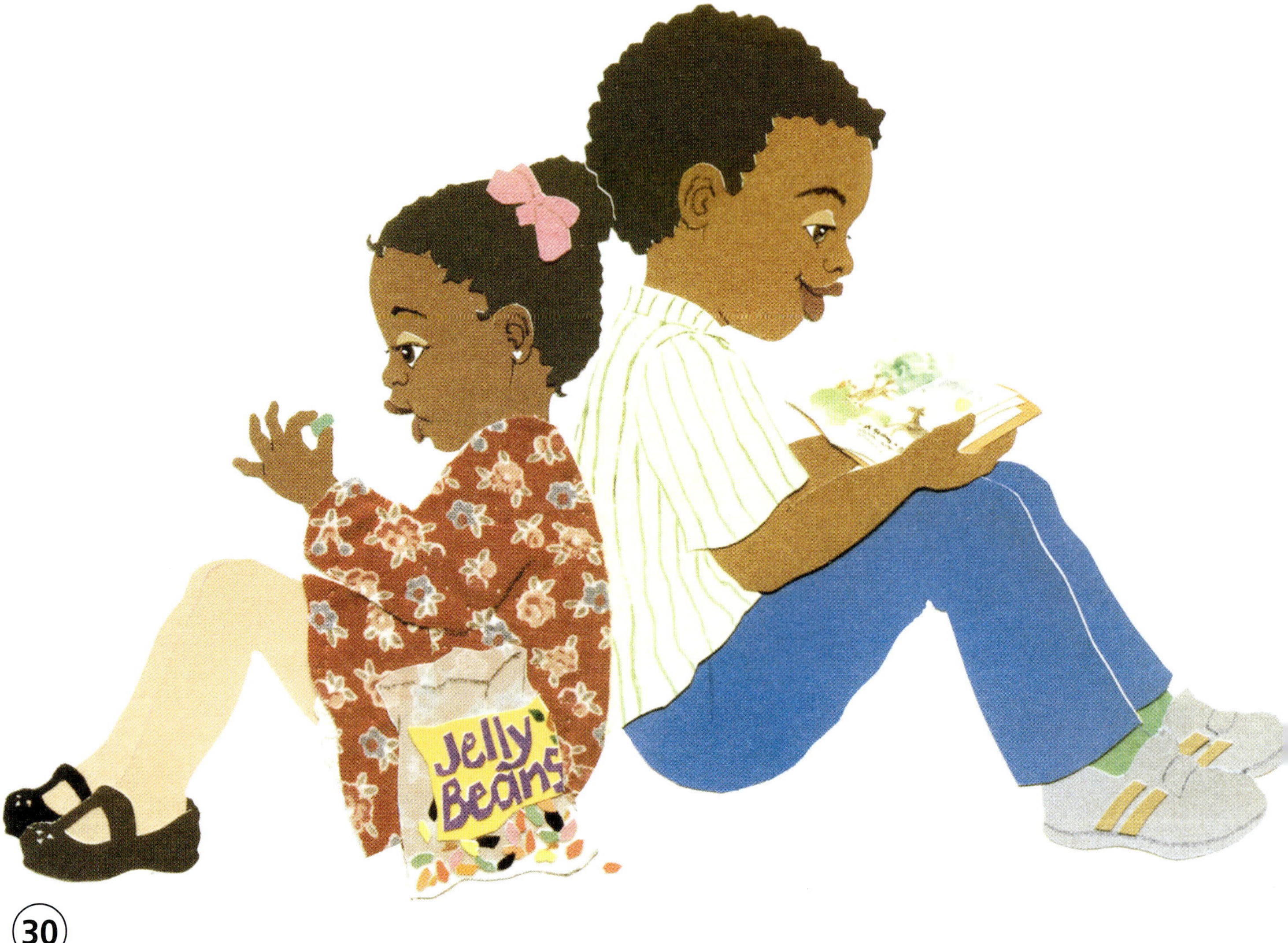
Jelly
Beans